Christmas 1990

From
Auggie

How's Business?

How's Business?

by Barbara Baskin
and Karen Harris

illustrated by
Laura Hartman

Holt, Rinehart and Winston / New York

Published simultaneously in Canada by Holt, Rinehart
and Winston of Canada, Limited.
Printed in the United States of America
Designed by Victoria Gomez
10 9 8 7 6 5 4 3 2 1

Library of Congress Cataloging in Publication Data
Baskin, Barbara Holland, 1929–
How's business?
Summary: An illustrated collection of jokes similar to the "knock-knock" variety, such as: "I'm in the poultry business." "How's business?" "Fowl!"
1. Wit and humor, Juvenile. 2. American wit and humor. [1. Jokes] I. Harris, Karen H., 1934–
II. Hartman, Laura, ill. III. Title.
PN6163.B3 818'.5402 81-13234
ISBN 0-03-060539-3 AACR2

ISBN 0-03-060539-3

To Myra, Seth, David, Julie,
Bruce, Amy and Michael *BB and KH*

For Vittorio *LH*

I'm in the bakery business.
How's business?

I'm making lots of dough!

I’m in the elevator business.
How’s business?

It has its ups and downs!

I’m in the tennis business.
How’s business?

It’s a real racquet!

I'm in the janitor business.
How's business?

I'm cleaning up!

I'm in the dressmaking business.
How's business?

Sew-sew!

I'm in the marble business.
How's business?

Everyone takes it for granite!

I'm in the toboggan business.
How's business?

It's going downhill!

I'm in the camera business.
How's business?

It's a snap!

I'm in the solar exploration business.
How's business?

Far out!

I'm in the window business.
How's business?

It's a pane!

I'm in the health food business.
How's business?

It's a natural!

I'm in the library business.
How's business?

I'm all booked up!

I'm in the cat breeding business.
How's business?

Purrfect!

I'm in the pillow business.
How's business?

It's getting me down!

I'm in the teaching business.
How's business?

It's got class!

I'm in the abacus business.
How's business?

You can count on it!

I'm in the drill business.
How's business?

Boring!

I'm in the fireplace business.
How's business?

Grate!

I'm in the traffic court business.
How's business?

Fine!

I'm in the trampoline business.
How's business?

Really jumping!

I'm in the firecracker business.
How's business?

Booming!

I'm in the tool business.
How's business?

It's awl right!

I'm in the archaeology business.
How's business?

In ruins!

I'm in the golf business.
How's business?

Suits me to a tee!

I'm in the rooster business.
How's business?

Nothing to crow about!

I'm in the sheepherding business.
How's business?

Baaaaaaad!

I'm in the medium business.
How's business?

My spirits are high!

I'm in the football business.
How's business?

I get a kick out of it!

I'm in the poultry business.
How's business?

Fowl!

I'm in the aqualung business.
How's business?

I can't keep my head above water!

I'm in the catering business.
How's business?

It takes the cake!

I'm in the kennel business.
How's business?

Going to the dogs!

I'm in the boat business.
How's business?

Sails are up!

I'm in the flagpole sitting business.
How's business?

Falling off!

I'm in the disc jockey business.
How's business?

I set new records every week!

I'm in the plumbing business.
How's business?

Going down the drain!

I'm in the doctor business.
How's business?

It requires a lot of patients!

I'm in the poetry business.
How's business?

Could be verse!

I'm in the author business.
How's business?

It's all write!

I'm in the air-conditioning business.
How's business?

Cool!

I'm in the fish business.
How's business?

Floundering!

I'm in the soap business.
How's business?

I'm cleaning up!

I'm in the ballet business.
How's business?

It keeps me on my toes!

I'm in the bicycle business.
How's business?

I'm a big wheel!

I’m in the tree surgery business.
How’s business?

I’m boughing out!

I'm in the auto racing business.
How's business?

It's a drag!

I'm in the yardstick business.
How's business?

Good, as a rule!

I'm in the perfume business.
How's business?

I haven't made a scent!

I'm in the astronomy business.
How's business?

Looking up!

I'm in the coal business.
How's business?

It's all mine!

I'm in the soccer business.
How's business?

I can't kick!

I'm in the glue business.
How's business?

I'll stick with it!

I'm in the telephone business.
How's business?

I'm a big operator!

I'm in the coffee business.
How's business?

It's bean good to me!

I'm in the real estate business.
How's business?

I like it a lot!

I'm in the exterminator business.
How's business?

I'm still working the bugs out of it!

I'm in the housekeeping business.
How's business?

Picking up!

I'm in the X-ray business.
How's business?

I'm still looking for the big break!

I'm in the diamond business.
How's business?

I don't carat all for it!

I'm in the pencil business.
How's business?

It has its points!

I'm in the tailoring business.
How's business?

Suits me!

I'm in the tennis business.
How's business?

I LOVE it!

I'm in the quilting business.
How's business?

It's a great comfort!

I'm in the music business.
How's business?

You've got to B sharp!

I'm in the service station business.
How's business?

It's a gas!

I'm in the gardening business.
How's business?

I dig it!

I'm in the drum business.
How's business?

I get a bang out of it!

I'm in the cardiology business.
How's business?

My heart's not in it!

I'm in the bowling business.
How's business?

It's right down my alley!

I'm in the weather forecasting business.
How's business?

It's a breeze!

I'm in the barbering business.
How's business?

It's been one close shave after another!

I'm in the undertaking business.
How's business?

Very grave!

I'm in the watch repair business.
How's business?

I got in it at the right time!

I'm in the psychiatry business.
How's business?

A lot of people are a-Freud of it!

I'm in the banking business.
How's business?

It's a big change for me!

I'm in the optician business.
How's business?

I'm trying not to make a spectacle of myself!

I'm in the wallpaper business.
How's business?

It's driving me up the wall!

I'm in the cattle raising business.
How's business? I said, How's business?

I herd, I herd!

I'm in the lighting business.
How's business?

It's got a bright future!

I'm in the road repair business.
How's business?

In a rut!

I'm in the classical song business.
How's business?

We need a new leider!

I'm in the fiction publishing business.
How's business?

Looking for novel ways to make money!

I'm in the computer business.
How's business?

BASICally great!

I'm in the yeast business.
How's business?

You'd get a rise out of it!

I'm in the Renaissance art business.
How's business?

I'm going baroque!

I'm in the circus business.
How's business?

I clown around a lot!

I'm in the genetics business.
How's business?

I clone around a lot!

I'm in the secretarial business.
How's business?

It's not my type *of profession!*

I'm in the pig food business.
How's business?

Just swill!

I'm in the salad business.
How's business?

Lettuce not discuss it!

I'm in the snail raising business.
How's business?

Slow!

I'm in the snake collecting business.
How's business?

Don't asp!

I'm in the allergy business.
How's business?

Nothing to sneeze at!

I'm in the fried food business.
How's business?

It isn't panning out!

I'm in the coin minting business.
How's business?

Nice, for a change!

I'm in the dairy business.
How's business?

MOO-ving along!

I'm in the psychoanalysis business.
How's business?

It's a dream!

I'm in the ophthalmology business.
How's business?

Eye like it!

I'm in the pickle business.
How's business?

I relish my job!

I'm in the parasol business.
How's business?

A shade better than last year!

I'm in the railroad business.
How's business?

Hard to keep track of!

I'm in the rabbit breeding business.
How's business?

It's a hare-raising venture!

I'm in the hotel business.
How's business?

I'd only recommend it as a last resort!

I'm in the séance business.
How's business?

Good, when the spirit moves me!

I'm in the strongbox business.
How's business?

Pretty safe!

I'm in the army food business.
How's business?

It's a mess!

I'm in the arrow packaging business.
How's business?

It's got me all aquiver!

I'm in the coronation business.
How's business?

It's all rite!

I'm in the folktale collecting business.
How's business?

Grimm!

I'm in the piano-playing business.
How's business?

Sonata so good!

I'm in the macrame business.
How's business?

Knot what you'd expect!

I'm in the antelope business.
How's business?

There's really nothing gnu!

I'm in the hangman business.
How's business?

I'm at the end of my rope!

I'm in the dental hygienist business.
How's business?

You have to brush up on a lot of stuff!

I'm in the poison ivy medicine business.
How's business?

We've had a rash of new orders recently!

I'm going into the transport business.
How's business?

I don't know; I'm still in training!

I'm in the broom business.
How's business?

Great. Our products are sweeping the country!

I'm in the blacksmith business.
How's business?

We're forging ahead!

I'm in the tea raising business.
How's business?

I can take it or leaf it!

I'm in the marathon supply business.
How's business?

We give people a run for their money!

I'm in the florist business.
How's business?

Rosy!

I'm in the philately business.
How's business?

Our competition is trying to stamp us out!

I'm in the mutiny business.
How's business?

Revolting!

I'm in the tobacco business.
How's business?

My profits are going up in smoke!

I'm in the umpire business.
How's business?

I just don't know the score!

I'm in the dictionary business.
How's business?

I just can't find the words to tell you!

I'm in the insect business.
How's business?

It's the little things about it that bug me!

About the Authors

BARBARA BASKIN and KAREN HARRIS are in the professor business, Baskin at the State University of New York and Harris at the University of New Orleans. Through a happy accident of birth, professors Baskin and Harris shared the same parents. While children, they participated in family marathons of punning, and so prepared themselves for writing this book. Together, they have managed to publish many articles and to write or edit four professional books.

About the Illustrator

LAURA HARTMAN is a graduate of the High School of Music and Art and the Cooper Union in New York City. She worked as a commercial artist, and designed handicrafts, kits, and toys before turning full time to illustration. She has illustrated *Your Burro Is No Jackass!*, *Alvin Fernald, TV Anchorman,* and *The Wacky World of Alvin Fernald.*

About the Book

The line illustrations for *How's Business?* were drawn on plate-finish Strathmore paper, using crow-quill and technical pens.